Book of
Failed Salvation

Poems

Julia Knobloch

Ben Yehuda Press
Teaneck, New Jersey

Published by Ben Yehuda Press
122 Ayers Court #1B
Teaneck, NJ 07666

http://www.BenYehudaPress.com

Jewish Poetry Project #20
http://jpoetry.us

To subscribe to our monthly book club and support independent Jewish publishing, visit https://www.patreon.com/BenYehudaPress

ISBN13 978-1-953829-15-3

21 22 23 / 10 9 8 7 6 5 4 3 2 1   20211117

שחר אבקשך

At dawn, I seek You

-Shlomo Ibn Gabirol

Contents

PORT OF SALT, IN THE WEST

for Yehuda Halevi

This port was founded when the temple stood
in the east, across the sea

Phoenicians salted fish; Romans traded pottery
when the temple fell in the east, across the sea

From this port of salt you embarked
driven by your longing for the dawn

fallen kingdoms behind you, waiting for you
in the east, across the sea

Far is the green river from this port of salt
Your daughter and her son stood on the quay

They promised to tend your empty gardens
You fell into the dust at the gates of your desire

Please call me Morenica, one more time
The sun has turned my pale skin dark

Your ship sails to the east, across the sea
and all my longing goes with you, Yehuda

IN THE DESERT

Before I left for the desert I dropped you off
at the house of study
I can't locate on the map
I remember the street
hibiscus bushes in front of the library
and how you texted me directions
together with the photo we took.

I got lost on my way out of the city
I didn't mind
I didn't look at the directions
I enjoyed the detour through the valley
a few extra moments in this foreign place
where the license plate made me a native.

Earlier that day, when I parked the car
to meet you for eggs and salads and coffee at the Café 7
a woman called out from the sidewalk:
There is space!
And this was promising because in Hebrew
it also meant: There is G-d!
And seven is a promising number
as promising as your name
although your name
has been appropriated by alien gods.

I was not a native.
Before I left for the desert I wanted a photo
with a panoramic view although the panoramic view
makes it look like the city weren't ours, too.
And because we were friends

we took it fast, as if not to linger long
but you can see
what would happen after the desert
you can see it in the space between our bodies.

And in the background, you don't see the city at all
only cypresses and barbed wire.

INHERITANCE

My olive harvest was destroyed and the moon stood high over Yaffa Road
Why take a photo, my companion asked.
Behold the moment, enjoy the night.

Shabbat was over.
From the doorway of a small shul near the shuk
light fell into a quiet, new week of dates and jasmine.

We sang of gold and roses.
After bare and sour pilgrimage, there was time
for one more pomegranate juice; for salvation, a few hours.

At dawn, I drove down silent hills,
I beheld the parting moon leading me into the morning.
Stranger in exile, she said, I will come back and so will you—

Julia Knobloch

YEDID NEFESH

Light washes over kitchen tiles like water
wavering with the rhythm of the trees

Sometimes I don't remember if your eyes
are green or amber, eyes of a deer

Where we are from
deer are symbols of male splendor

swift and strong
Far from the land, they hide

in birch forests, behind dark pines
Come quick, I want to feel your heart beat

return to our embrace

Dew was in your hair when I left
the tiles in your apartment cool under my feet

tea glasses and date syrup on the kitchen table
quiet olive trees outside

I am up early again this morning
the water called me to the beach

Where you are now, the world is still asleep

AT DAWN

After Jacob and the Angel, *by Yehuda Amichai*

You will return to the east at the height of summer
already the fans in my apartment are turning fast
at dawn
I can't stop thinking about the poem you sent

I tan my skin
my swimsuit leaves white lines for you
to see and touch the way a humid summer does
slowly, oblivious to age

Time is marked
by the appearance of morning purple and fire flies
by when to water the plants
another flask of sunscreen a new week

The city turns into a village by the sea

In the grocery store the label *Grown in California* makes me grin
I buy an extra pint of berries for good measure
as a charm
the last word from you I have is *yes*, all caps
but the weather forecast is not always accurate

I keep thinking of the poem you sent
imagine that long wave coming to the shore
I water the plants

I spot another flower on the vine
Soon you might be in this garden, too

Julia Knobloch

At dawn
you might let me go, into the lurking autumn of my body
Do we even need to struggle? You already know my name

TAMMUZ

It was a day from childhood summers
when you could stay inside
without the urgency to seize the day
when there would always be more of this—
this heat, this scent, these cherries
when you could still go to the beach tomorrow and again.

The sunset turned brownstones yellow.
We sat in my glowing garden
one day and fifty years after the landing on the moon.
An ocher crescent waxed on the label of the wine you brought.

I stroked your naked feet that rested in my lap.
Your eyes were green and amber.

One day and nineteen hundred fifty years ago,
the city's walls were breached.
I was supposed to guard the temple courts—
how could I not yield to summer's siege?

Julia Knobloch

HAVDALAH ON DITMARS BOULEVARD

We walked underneath the railroad bridge,
its arcs shaped like vaults of a cathedral

You wondered if it was permissible to compare them to the tablets
A tree grew in the open space

Late sunlight hovered over water and in the park, long shadows
From somewhere came the smell of barbecue. The city didn't know
it would wake up to the first chilly August morning of the year

A hidden path led from Palestine to Greece
The waitress brought us dessert,
to celebrate the love she thought she saw

We walked to the corner arm in arm.
Underneath three stars you said it was time
for me to board the train,
to leave behind light and contentment of the seventh day—
the world now made of only ordinary days
filled with words I don't understand, a blessing and a curse

FAILED SALVATION

Now that summer is over and we're not lovers any more, I lost the few pounds I wanted to lose before the summer, before you undressed me on a humid thunderstorm night in July, the hottest night of the summer, when it wasn't clear whether G-d was celebrating or raging. You suggested that maybe Hashem wasn't happy and I, who had been waiting for you as for a savior, wanting to see your face again, your chest hair framed by an adobe colored V-neck, knowing that soon I would know you *in the Biblical sense*, I laughed and said, Oh no, Hashem is happy, when it should have given me pause that the rainfall was apocalyptic and it was too dark for even a rainbow. After our fight one day after your birthday you wrote you had been thinking a lot about our connection over the past weeks, months, and years, and I have done the same. I have thought a lot about the Shabbat lunch one February where we first met, you in a red t-shirt and a scarf loosely wrapped around your neck, looking like a proud, tight-lipped Zionist. You made a disparaging comment about the people of the country I was born in but friended me on Facebook a couple days later and invited me to a dinner, and although I had been hoping for you to be in touch I declined to go, with a half-hearted excuse that was only half a lie, because I worried I might fall in love with you and that there were too many years between us. I have thought of the evening at the start-up Talmud class, when I felt your glance, your earnest, guarded glance, warm and curious, that I noticed again at the retreat up the Hudson, when you lay stretched out on the floor and I looked at you when I walked out of the room. Or one year later, when I gave a sermon about the nature of love and salvation and spotted you among the crowd. Or a week after the humid July thunderstorm night when, on the sofa in my kitchen, you made a vague attempt to caress my cheek, which I took for shyness then, but now for regret and pity. That night I noticed for the first time that your eyes are both green and amber. Funny, right, I always remembered the intensity of your glance and not the color of your eyes. Looking back there was something hesitant in

Julia Knobloch

your behavior already on that dark, humid thunderstorm night, almost imperceptible, faint enough to be almost washed away with the rain, and maybe it was for this undefined hesitant something, not for the few pounds I had not yet lost that I felt as undesirable as never before, full of desire that felt undesired, inhibited, age-inappropriate, and angry about it, angry at me, at you, at my body, our wrong decisions. I have thought about the night in early August, when our bodies were so close I thought I felt your soul, when you asked, Is this good? And it was good. Where was the last time I saw you, you asked when we met up in the spring, before the summer, when we were still friends, which was good, too, and we both said, Washington Square, and smiled. It was your birthday, I had an interview the next day, and you had invited friends to hang out on a humid late August day in Washington Square Park. The next day, the day after your birthday, you texted me good energy right before the interview, and if a psychic had told us I'd be yelling at you on 6th Avenue exactly one year later we would not have believed it. Near the Garibaldi statue we hugged good-bye, our hands running down each other's arm, our fingers just so delaying the separation, and I have been thinking a lot about the look on your face that day. Now, the last time I saw you was in front of the Brooklyn Public Library looming against a black sky. Summer was over and we were not lovers anymore, and instead of giving me a hug, you gave a blessing of sorts, of which I only understood "May you be," before you stopped half-way and turned around. As I watched your blue kippah disappear among the crowd, I thought of our intentions, profusely discussed over the previous weeks, to remain friends, to become even better friends than before, maybe, someday. I thought of how you once said you didn't relate to the idea of embodying salvation, of creating salvation together, and I may have understood why you said that and what you meant, then again, I believe it is something people can do, maybe the only thing we can do, save one another on nights too dark for even a rainbow—because what else is love if not salvation?

WHAT WAS I EVEN THINKING?

After In the Middle of This Century, *by Yehuda Amichai*

August is a slowly aging woman
like Av, a two-faced month
leading the way to fall and renewal
to the end of the summer I thought
this one would be—
then again, what kind of summer
did I even think this one would be?

A summer that would last all but three weeks
the last before the long goodbye
to my tanned flesh and mortal hips
to songs we might have sung
to a white moon in the Levant.

Wild geese are flying and the cicada
in the tree outside my window
sings louder, early.
I hear of comfort happening to people.

The prophet saw the shatnez of our mingling
lost in translation and desire—
too many years between us
your journey to another land.

You want to leave in peace.
I want to write your name with love.
I want to speak in praise of your transient face
that I touched when you were near
with full eyes, for a short while.

Julia Knobloch

SHA'AREI HESED

The moon is new and your seat is empty
I remember how you sat here
wounded like a lonely city
I turned my back to you as if I didn't care

wishing you would teach me
from the book for imperfect people
in the language you speak well
like you did one night

that was complete as a city at noon
under date palms

At dawn, I wanted to kiss your forehead
You turned your closed eyes to the wall and I forgot

to say the prayer for the road

The city was brisk and brilliant, like your mind

NEW YEAR

The world is in suspension like the sky this morning.
The lights from Tony's deli that kept me up
after the floor lamp had gone out
keep blinking, seemingly weaker than during the night.
A truck idles at the intersection. A car races down the avenue.

Words of remorse and faith will soon be chanted
while the shuttle passes by
the open windows of the synagogue,
the sound of the new year ripping through the neighborhood
like fire trucks or Sarah's laughter.

Summer is a bygone decade.

You live a block from here but for the holiday you have left town.
You will wake up under the same undecided sky.

Last night—which was today, depending on how you measure—
my friends and I walked on Eastern Parkway,
the lamps in many houses were still on,
a faint smell of fire in the air.
Bare legs and fading tan, we didn't go down your block guessing
which of the dark windows was yours.

SUMMER SOLSTICE IN JOSHUA TREE PARK

When I first heard about the trees I didn't know
that scientists say they soon might disappear
because the desert has become too hot.
In the east, I dreamed of places I had not seen
of times when traveling seemed a birthright
when I owned miles and years
when life didn't seem to run out before the summer solstice.
The days were getting longer but not warmer
the sun moved forward present but unseen.
It was late when I reached out to you
bold enough to hope you might have love for me
and make the sun stand still, yet weary
I dragged one night's magic into glaring light
and tainted it with lies about cheap pleasure.
In the east, the streets were wet and the truth was cold.
I didn't find what I was looking for. I saw the trees out west.

MAGICAL THINKING

Clouds over the mountain, the sun is strong before a thunderstorm.
I always feel embraced by humid air, part of the world and time.
Of the songs I wrote, you liked one about memories that seep
into the fabric of an old summer house. You called it magical.

The reader said there are bonds between us from past lives unresolved.
One time, you wanted to return and then you couldn't,
another time, we belonged to the same academy.
The reader said she saw sandals, the word *Israel*.

When I wear sandals, I think of you. Your studies and your laughter.
I always trusted your advice even when I didn't follow your directions.

Now I don't know where you are and where you're headed.
Past life bonds are crutches for those who can't let go.
One night, your foot was hurt. I didn't pay attention.
The reader said healing couldn't happen.
Do you believe in the world to come?

MAR READS THE I-CHING

We close the book of the desert and Mar reads me the I-Ching
in her Berber tent near the quarry, in the woods.
The weak lines are a good sign, she says,
a glow from yellow candles on her face.
Ritual tames excessive creativity, she says, and I cry
because I know she is right.
There is truth in repetition.
We drink champagne from Albuquerque and speak of cottonwoods
of the Hudson River and the Rio Grande
of leaving the desert and looking back.
Mar asks if I can hear the owl.
Rivers don't flow where I'm going,
nearby are arroyos and bizarre rocks, chilly nights, coyotes.
The promised land is a desert with almond trees.

LEAVING NEW YORK IV

And suddenly the vines around my window frame—
Like every year I wasn't home when they unfurled.
The garden calls me early to look for purple flowers.
Will I live with just the memory?
How can I touch the orange glow that fills my kitchen?

And suddenly the rain, not a surprise, still unforeseen—
Like every year I want to run on warm asphalt,
feet naked, my dress soaked.
Secrets of the world are tangible in heat and rain.
Master of the universe, don't ever let me die!

And suddenly the city, island in the sun—
Like a lover eyeing the July sky, a leaf of grass between his lips.
I wish to touch his curls again and hear him speak about his life.
He is a harbor, not a shoreline.
I wish there had been time to say goodbye.

Julia Knobloch

SHABBAT EKEV

The air feels like spring or fall, the yards like fairy tales
of Spanish bungalows, sleeping beauties under plantain plants.
Next to a pomegranate tree, three cypresses tower into the sky.

I miss Prospect Park, the meadow opening toward the ocean.
I used to stride straight through it, like an explorer, or gusts of wind.
Here, the parks are pretty lawns, not a drop of sweat runs down my
back.

Past the empty intersection, the hills remind me of another East,
ahead the west is a backlit orange blur.
It's been one year since I walked in this dress, these sandals.

What's unplanned can seem prophetic, meaningful in arbitrariness
like my walking now where you once lived,
in the clothes I wore when I knew I had to change.

These are weeks of consolation.
Though my hair is flat and my skin dry, I will be happy here.
Intentions can cause outcomes, an ever-lasting bond.

I came to turn unlived love into something new, maybe even holy.
I will, but it is difficult, to live a broader love when the empty world
is beautiful and self-sufficient, meaningful in arbitrariness.

MY CURRENT PROMISED LAND

At dawn, when I face east and cypresses, I smell the ocean
In the stillness of the heat I hear the palm tree creaking

dates dropping on cement. Blinds clatter
when night falls with the temperature, fragments of Hebrew

fill my room, the song of crickets, not cicadas
I caress each new book on the bamboo shelves

Another city lies beyond my street's retrofitted buildings
my previous encampments are within me, far away

I say their names out loud to remember how I got here
and where to go, I wonder if we or the heavens choose

when to close one circle and start another

I recall my last walk down the slope, past spread-out tables
and makeshift shelters lit by colored bulbs, adorned with flowers

like sukkahs sprinkled across the neighborhood before their time

How free I felt in my solitude before departure
How free the diners seemed, restricted by a new-won liberty

outside, underneath canopies and flimsy tarps
tranquility afforded by an emergency response

Julia Knobloch

BIRTHDAY POEM

The waters are a constant roar, the hills seem close today.
Winged birds of all kinds in the sky, the tide is rising.
It makes me laugh, to dive into the shining swirl,
I jump and splash, everything is very good
on this fifth day of the week.
Man and woman created you in winter like Hashem created
light and darkness, beach and trees and man and woman,
male and female created He them.
I may never know you in that sense again
or find your amber eyes among the waves—
I love this world as I love you
there is no difference, David knew this well before me.
Maybe that is why he sometimes leapt and danced all by himself
then sashayed home, to play the lyre and write a poem.

HANCOCK PARK

In the space between our words are words I want to say
things I want continued

Each step we make toward preserving our history
on this heat-record breaking morning

in this historic residential neighborhood
is a step away from what is gone

And true, it's what I said I want to do, and true
you look strikingly familiar, in a dusk pink shirt and sun hat

while you read to me of people who once lived here
notice architectural complexities around us

while sprinklers irrigate the quiet lawn I stand on
because I can't stand closer than six feet to you

while I eat the sliced peach you brought and try to read your eyes

I want to listen to you always and say the things I cannot say

Julia Knobloch

COURTYARDS OF JERUSALEM

And there was not a courtyard in Jerusalem that was
not illuminated by the light of the Bet Hashoevah
—Mishna Sukkah

Eleven weeks went by
Three and seven and this last one
Before the sealing

You wished me well, that I should find a home
I felt at home with you
There is love in what you give

Impermanence, imagined memories
A time for everything
We are commanded to rejoice

Hills of Italy and Greece and Israel
Surround the cove
Days from the east return

A morning on Yannai Street
Four or two thousand years ago
One evening before Sukkot

My friend draws water from the lake
As she did one year, a world ago
In a Berkshire night

On our procession through the woods
Her voice led us past roots and pits
A torch, a pilgrim's moon

A map of ancient alleys
Stairs and yards anticipating joy
Light from worn-out priestly clothes

ROXBURY PARK

Now the last time I saw you was under a tree
at the breezy time of day
before we hugged and walked to our separate cars.
I couldn't touch your cheek beneath the mask
so I caressed the tree's thin, long leaves
wanting to know, again, why you won't love me
and as before, I thought, your silence shields me;
you once said yourself
you, too, hurt people, that time I cried
over someone else although I already liked you.
In this new place, the old must go, accept
completion over splendor—
Behold, not every couple builds an arc
that reaches from the west coast to the Levant.

Julia Knobloch

ON THE FOURTH DAY

They say the heat is coming, the winds that can bring fire,
winds that blew through the detective novels of my youth.
I forget what month it is but I know the seasons change
by the course of sunlight on the balcony.
Last week I drove to a beach through rugged hills,
the kind of beach that blows the past away.
I forget what time zone I am in,
my friends, how will they spend the winter, my parents,
confined to spend their precious, shorter days inside.
I want to turn the clock back more than just one hour.
Last night, the full moon of the month they say is bitter
peeked past the shingles of the bungalow next door
through my California blinds, alluding to redemption,
peeked like it did in a book my father used to read me
about two children who travel to the moon
whose northern face still looked as I remembered.

LA CIENEGA PARK

The 24th of Kislev was about to end, dusk was falling
I recognized your face

from more than four cubits away, six feet

You wore blue and I wore green
We sat down on a white bench

near the playground of your youth
One by one the children left

stars came out and darkness settled in
You said the words I needed you to say

Your arms around me
beneath your light down coat, your heart

that will love someone else

As we parted ways to kindle light and sing
the blessing for having reached this point in time

you called out to me—*This piece of garment
on the ground, does it belong to you?* It didn't

Hefker, you said and smiled, maybe you did
Maybe I smiled

Hefker, like us, I thought
We are lost, we are set free, we can be claimed by anyone

Julia Knobloch

EXIT

We have fulfilled our obligation to mend the past

The stars were right
Ours is not a lucky constellation although at times

I hoped we might yet drink from champagne jugs
because I don't know the exact hour of your birth

There is nothing I can do against words
spoken in a city of prophets

When we exited the tavern, you blew a kiss
to the singer and the streets fell silent

In the house of the priestess I contemplated
your delicate face

I miss your curious gaze

AND FROM THIS WE LEARN

After "At the Stone of Losses" by T. Carmi

Sunlight on ocher stones, in an empty city
I wait for you by the Time Elevator. Silent
you walk toward me. You wave your hand

Underneath a white umbrella with yellow stripes
your smile is still the smile I conjured up each time
you veiled the anger in your eyes with laughter

In a musty limestone backyard sprinkled with weeds
you sit lost, caught in circles. I can't reclaim you
anymore, although I merited a chance

although the sages taught to cease prayers for rain
only when rising waters obscure the Claimant's Stone

Days are torrid
Even the crows have left

In the purple distance, east winds are flaring
The umber summit looks like a volcano

Julia Knobloch

WEST COAST

When I was young I laughed a lot
So many pictures of me laughing
To be around your laughter, your earnest eyes
There are too many white cars in LA
I wish my friend were still alive
Mountains hold these blocks together, built on tar and oil
boarded-up stores and white-washed windows
empty, dry and dry and empty
When the sky is overcast, palm trees look like forgotten props
I have not forgotten my first blizzard on Tenth Avenue
I kiss my plants goodnight
I don't know how your skin smells in the morning
Since Queens I have not been with anyone
I left the east during a hurricane, I saw my friends down at the beach
The plane would not crash, with my friends down at the beach
I had your postcard with me, and the chocolates
I don't overestimate you
Unrequited displays of esteem are awkward
You might have always been afraid of me
Would that I had known to show you that I saw
your tenderness
let you see mine
It would not have made you love me
It could have helped build trust, or friendship
One hundred years later
I only thought about caressing your pained face
I still do
One ocean and one continent, a European at what once was
the last American frontier, her back against the sea
The temple was destroyed because of carelessness
People weren't in touch with feelings

Or too much
The ways I've been abandoned, if you had known
I wonder if I could have made you happy
I wanted to
Please forgive my carelessness
I was too insecure
I loved your sandals
I loved to see your hair curl up
I loved that you are tall
I loved your intense cautiousness, your quiet curiosity
I loved your love for ritual, for song, for beauty

It is not in the heavens. There is no other choice than choosing life.

WESTWOOD

This corner was your corner
it still is; will always be
The traffic lights could never change
fast enough when I drove west, against the sun
backlit palm trees and this sky here
that turns wide late in the afternoons

Three months, the best place in Los Angeles
I'd cut through the yard, skip over succulents
prickly shadows swaying
Behind the screen-door, you

Fesenjoon and raw carrots, always
a rest of ice-cream in the freezer, sparkling water
Your thoughts on paper strewn across the floor
vintage posters on the walls, askew
Please sit, eat, have some more
Your smile
Slant light in the staircase
Your bedroom door ajar

We did not keep our promises
The house is gone, but we are here
crossed-legged on oriental cushions
debating what it means to look forward to the days of old

Julia Knobloch

Notes

Yedid Nefesh	"Beloved of the Soul", love poem/song traditionally sung on the Jewish Sabbath
Tammuz	Month on the Hebrew calendar
Havdalah	Ritual that separates the Jewish Sabbath from the rest of the week
Av	Month on the Hebrew calendar
Shatnez	Term for the biblically prohibited mix of wool and linen
Sha'arei Hesed	"Gates of Kindness", neighborhood in Jerusalem
Shabbat Ekev	Ekev is a Torah portion, usually read in August. Ekev is often translated as "because."
Sukkahs	Booths used during the Jewish Festival of Tabernacles
Hefker	A Jewish legal term describing the status of lost things

Acknowledgements

Inheritance is included as Erev Sukkot in *Do Not Return*, published by Broadstone Books, 2019

What Was I Even Thinking was published with ritualwell.org

Leaving New York IV and Magical Thinking (as Sandals from the Past) were published in *When We Turned Within, Reflections on COVID-19*, edited by Rabbi Menachem Creditor and Sarah Tuttle-Singer

My Current Promised Land was published in print and online with the *Los Angeles Jewish Journal*

Birthday Poem was published as On the Fifth Day with ritualwell.org

About the Author

Julia Knobloch is a poet and rabbi-in-training at the Ziegler School for Rabbinic Studies in Los Angeles. In 2021, she was awarded a Bruce Geller Memorial Prize/AJU Word Grant to support her creative work at the intersection of poetry, midrash, and liturgy.

She double-majored in Philosophy and Romance Languages with a Magister Artium degree from Heidelberg University, Germany and has lived in France, Portugal, and Argentina.

A 2018 Brooklyn Poets Fellow, her poems can be found online as well as in print magazines and anthologies.

Her debut poetry collection *Do Not Return* was published in 2019 by Broadstone Books.

The Jewish Poetry Project

jpoetry.us

Ben Yehuda Press

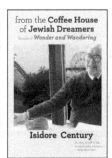

From the Coffee House of Jewish Dreamers: Poems of Wonder and Wandering and the Weekly Torah Portion by Isidore Century

"Isidore Century is a wonderful poet. His poems are funny, deeply observed, without pretension." – *The Jewish Week*

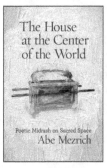

The House at the Center of the World: Poetic Midrash on Sacred Space by Abe Mezrich

"Direct and accessible, Mezrich's midrashic poems often tease profound meaning out of his chosen Torah texts. These poems remind us that our Creator is forgiving, that the spiritual and physical can inform one another, and that the supernatural can be carried into the everyday."
—Yehoshua November, author of *God's Optimism*

we who desire: Poems and Torah riffs by Sue Swartz

"Sue Swartz does magnificent acrobatics with the Torah. She takes the English that's become staid and boring, and adds something that's new and strange and exciting. These are poems that leave a taste in your mouth, and you walk away from them thinking, what did I just read? Oh, yeah. It's the Bible."
—Matthue Roth, author, *Yom Kippur A Go-Go*

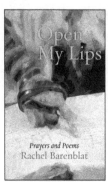

Open My Lips: Prayers and Poems
by Rachel Barenblat

"Barenblat's God is a personal God—one who lets her cry on His shoulder, and who rocks her like a colicky baby. These poems bridge the gap between the ineffable and the human. This collection will bring comfort to those with a religion of their own, as well as those seeking a relationship with some kind of higher power."
—Satya Robyn, author, *The Most Beautiful Thing*

Words for Blessing the World: Poems in Hebrew and English by Herbert J. Levine

"These writings express a profoundly earth-based theology in a language that is clear and comprehensible. These are works to study and learn from."
—Rodger Kamenetz, author, *The Jew in the Lotus*

Shiva Moon: Poems by Maxine Silverman

"The poems, deeply felt, are spare, spoken in a quiet but compelling voice, as if we were listening in to her inner life. This book is a precious record of the transformation saying Kaddish can bring."
—Howard Schwartz, author, *The Library of Dreams*

is: heretical Jewish blessings and poems by Yaakov Moshe (Jay Michaelson)

"Finally, Torah that speaks to and through the lives we are actually living: expanding the tent of holiness to embrace what has been cast out, elevating what has been kept down, advancing what has been held back, reveling in questions, revealing contradictions."
—Eden Pearlstein, aka eprhyme

Texts to the Holy: Poems
by Rachel Barenblat

"These poems are remarkable, radiating a love of God that is full bodied, innocent, raw, pulsating, hot, drunk. I can hardly fathom their faith but am grateful for the vistas they open. I will sit with them, and invite you to do the same."
—Merle Feld, author of *A Spiritual Life*

The Sabbath Bee: Love Songs to Shabbat
by Wilhelmina Gottschalk

"Torah, say our sages, has seventy faces. As these prose poems reveal, so too does Shabbat. Here we meet Shabbat as familiar housemate, as the child whose presence transforms a family, as a spreading tree, as an annoying friend who insists on being celebrated, as a woman, as a man, as a bee, as the ocean."
—Rachel Barenblat, author, *The Velveteen Rabbi's Haggadah*

All the Holes Line Up: Poems and Translations
by Zackary Sholem Berger

"Spare and precise, Berger's poems gaze unflinchingly at—but also celebrate—human imperfection in its many forms. And what a delight that Berger also includes in this collection a handful of his resonant translations of some of the great Yiddish poets." —Yehoshua November, author of *God's Optimism* and *Two World Exist*

How to Bless the New Moon: The Priestess Paths Cycle and Other Poems for Queens
by Rachel Kann

"To read Rachel Kann's poems is to be confronted with the possibility that you, too, are prophet and beloved, touched by forces far beyond your mundane knowing. So, dear reader, enter into the 'perfumed forcefield' of these words—they are healing and transformative."
—Rabbi Jill Hammer, co-author of *The Hebrew Priestess*

Into My Garden
by David Caplan

"The beauty of Caplan's book is that it is not polemical. It does not set out to win an argument or ask you whether you've put your tefillin on today. These gentle poems invite the reader into one person's profound, ambiguous religious experience."
—*The Jewish Review of Books*

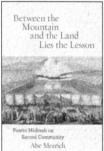

Between the Mountain and the Land is the Lesson: Poetic Midrash on Sacred Community
by Abe Mezrich

"Abe Mezrich cuts straight back to the roots of the Midrashic tradition, sermonizing as a poet, rather than idealogue. Best of all, Abe knows how to ask questions and avoid the obvious answers."
—Jake Marmer, author, *Jazz Talmud*

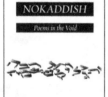

NOKADDISH: Poems in the Void
by Hanoch Guy Kaner

"A subversive, midrashic play with meanings—specifically Jewish meanings, and then the reversal and negation of these meanings."
—Robert G. Margolis

An Added Soul: Poems for a New Old Religion
by Herbert Levine

"These poems are remarkable, radiating a love of God that is full bodied, innocent, raw, pulsating, hot, drunk. I can hardly fathom their faith but am grateful for the vistas they open. I will sit with them, and invite you to do the same."
—Merle Feld, author of *A Spiritual Life*.

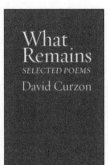

What Remains
by David Curzon

"Aphoristic, ekphrastic, and precise revelations animate WHAT REMAINS. In his stunning rewriting of Psalm 1 and other biblical passages, Curzon shows himself to be a fabricator, a collector, and an heir to the literature, arts, and wisdom traditions of the planet.
—Alicia Ostriker, author of *The Volcano and After*

The Shortest Skirt in Shul
by Sass Oron

"These poems exuberantly explore gender, Torah, the masks we wear, and the way our bodies (and the ways we wear them) at once threaten stable narratives, and offer the kind of liberation that saves our lives."
—Alicia Jo Rabins, author of *Divinity School*, composer of *Girls In Trouble*

Walking Triptychs
by Ilya Gutner

These are poems from when I walked about Shanghai and thought about the meaning of the Holocaust.

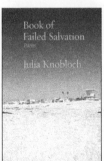

Book of Failed Salvation
by Julia Knobloch

"These beautiful poems express a tender longing for spiritual, physical, and emotional connection. They detail a life in movement—across distances, faith, love, and doubt."
—David Caplan, author, *Into My Garden*

CPSIA information can be obtained
at www.ICGtesting.com
Printed in the USA
LVHW030520261121
704408LV00001B/66